Welcome to: "Taylor Swift: Behind the Lyrics"

Dear Readers,

It is with great excitement that we invite you to embark on an extraordinary adventure into the world of Taylor Swift. This book is a tribute to her remarkable journey, a narrative woven with melodies, dreams, and determination.

Taylor Swift is not just a global superstar; she is a storyteller, a dreamer, and an inspiration to millions. Through her songs, she has touched hearts and narrated experiences that resonate with people of all ages. This book aims to bring you closer to Taylor's world, offering insights into her life, her music, and her legacy.

Inside these pages, you will find a detailed biography, intriguing facts, engaging puzzles, interactive quizzes, and motivational coloring pages — each element carefully crafted to celebrate Taylor's influence and creativity.

Whether you are a long-time Swiftie or new to her music, this journey promises to be enlightening, entertaining, and inspiring. As you turn each page, we hope you discover new aspects of Taylor's life and career, and perhaps, find a little bit of yourself in her stories.

So, grab your favorite pen or pencil, get comfortable, and let's dive into the captivating world of Taylor Swift!

The Fairytale begins.......

In the heart of Reading, Pennsylvania, on a chilly December 13th in 1989, a star was born. Taylor Alison Swift, an American singer-songwriter and actress, entered the world. Her journey into music began at the tender age of 12 when she started writing songs and learned to play the guitar. It was a love affair that would shape her life and the lives of millions around the globe.

.

This is the story of how an ordinary girl named Taylor Swift became a world-renowned country-pop sensation. As we move through her life in this chapter, you'll see that her path was not always smooth - it was lined with challenges and heartbreaks. But these experiences crafted her into the resilient artist she is today.

"In life, you learn lessons. And sometimes you learn them the hard way." Taylor Swift

.

Taylor Alison Swift was born on to Scott Kingsley Swift and Andrea Gardner Swift. Growing up on a Christmas tree farm instilled in young Taylor a deep connection with nature and inspired many lyrics in her future songs. Her first encounter with music came at an early age when she started playing guitar. A quote by Plato says "Music gives a soul to the universe," and for Taylor, music indeed became her soul.

In school, Taylor was often bullied but found solace in music as an escape from harsh reality. It's not surprising that most of her songs reflect themes of love, loss, friendship and adversity; they are drawn from real-life experiences which makes them so relatable.

Turning adversities into stepping stones is what led Taylor Swift from being bullied at school to becoming an international pop star

At just fourteen years old, she moved to Nashville with dreams of becoming a singer-songwriter. Nashville – known as Music City – was undoubtedly intimidating for such a young girl but also full of opportunities. The city's vibrant country scene allowed her talent to flourish.

"Fearless is getting back up and fighting for what you want over and over again... even though every time you've tried before, you've lost."
Taylor Swift

.

At just 16 years old, Swift released her self-titled debut album. The first single, "Tim McGraw," became an instant hit. Her rise to fame began when she signed with Big Machine Records in 2006 and released her self-titled debut album which hit number five on Billboard 200 chart within its first week! The secret to her success?

.

She poured personal experiences and stories into her lyrics. Her fans, affectionately known as "Swifties," found solace and connection in her storytelling.

Her many quotes throughout this book reflect Taylor Swift's wisdom, resilience, and positivity, which have resonated with her fans and made her a role model for many.

Swift's career shot up meteorically after that. Her second album "Fearless" won four Grammy Awards, making her the youngest Album of the Year winner. She transitioned smoothly from country to pop with her fifth album '1989,' proving her versatility and solidifying her place in the music industry.

Her journey wasn't without trials though. In 2016, Swift faced a series of personal setbacks including a public feud with Kim Kardashian and Kanye West which led to a year-long hiatus from public life. But she bounced back stronger than ever with her critically acclaimed sixth album 'Reputation.'

In these moments of adversity, Swift didn't shy away; instead, she poured all her feelings into creating magical melodies that resonated deeply with fans worldwide.

"Just be yourself, there is no one better." Taylor Swift

If you find yourself facing a hurdle in your quest for happiness/success like Taylor did, consider taking some time off to regroup and plan your comeback just as she did

Some of your thoughts…..

_____

_____

_____

_____

_____

Offstage, Swift is a cat lover with two feline companions named Olivia Benson and Meredith Grey after characters from popular TV shows. She's also known for her philanthropy - donating to various causes such as education and disaster relief. Advocacy for literacy is close to her heart; she has donated books to schools and libraries.

This isn't just about Taylor Swift's journey from a small-town girl to an international superstar; it's about how she uses her platform to make a difference. It's about her music, her life, and the impact she has on her fans. It's about the girl with a guitar who became a global phenomenon.

"No matter what happens in life, be good to people. Being good to people is a wonderful legacy to leave behind." Taylor Swift

Swift's story is an inspiration for anyone chasing their dreams – it shows us that no matter what adversities we face, we can always turn them into stepping stones towards our goals. After all, as Taylor herself once said: "No matter what happens in life, be good to people. Being good to people is a wonderful legacy to leave behind."

"People haven't always been there for me, but music always has." Taylor Swift

Think about…..

- Adversity can be turned into strength

- Swift's early exposure to music contributed significantly in shaping up her career

- At fourteen years old she went seeking opportunities and worked tirelessly towards achieving them.

Think about…..

- Despite reaching stardom at such young age, she continuously evolves as an artist

- When faced with tremendous challenges or backlash (like Swift's feud), taking some time off could help deal with the situation effective

Goal Achievement

Do you have dreams and goals you want to achieve? When you recognize the progress you've made and the support you've received along the way, you're more motivated to work towards your dreams.

What are your dreams:

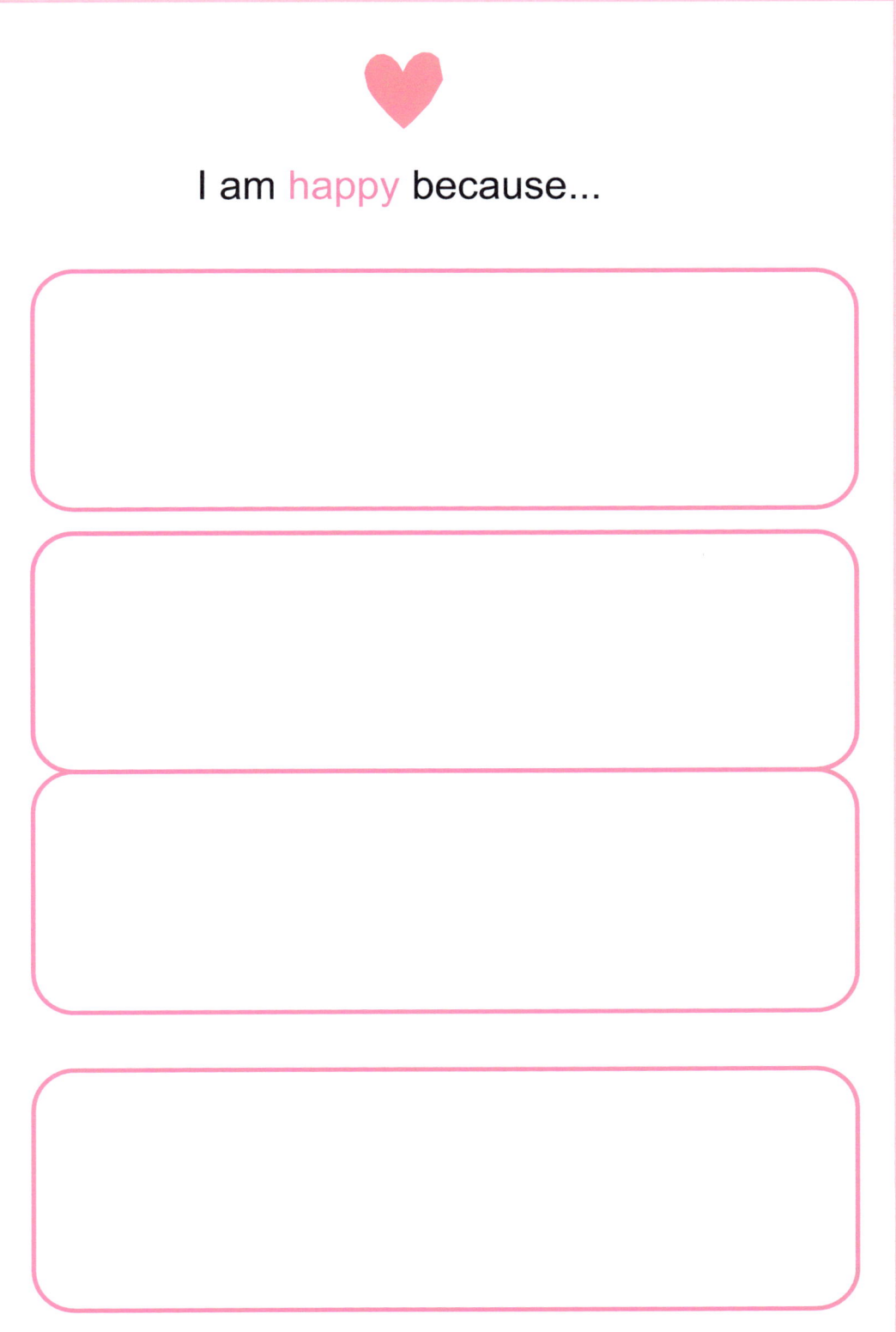

I am happy because...

I am Grateful for...

I am Planning to…….

My heart is full!

I will fill this heart with the things I am grateful for.

Date:

100 FACTS ABOUT TAYLOR SWIFT

Taylor Swift started writing songs at a very young age, around 12 years old.

She learned to play the guitar when she was 12, and it became one of her favorite instruments.

Taylor Swift's first album was self-titled, and it was released in 2006 when she was just 16 years old.

Her first single was "Tim McGraw," and it became a hit

100 FACTS ABOUT TAYLOR SWIFT

She often includes personal experiences and stories in her songs.

Taylor Swift is known for her storytelling lyrics, which resonate with her fans.

She has a close relationship with her fans, often referring to them as "Swifties."

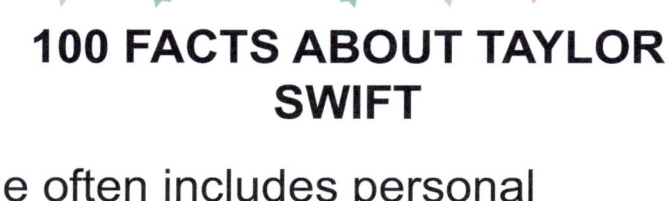

She has a song called "Mean," which sends a positive message about dealing with bullies.

100 FACTS ABOUT TAYLOR SWIFT

Taylor Swift's music spans multiple genres, including country, pop, and indie.

Her album "Fearless" won Album of the Year at the Grammy Awards in 2010.

Taylor Swift has a cat named Olivia Benson, named after a character from the TV show "Law & Order: SVU."

She is known for her signature red lipstick

100 FACTS ABOUT TAYLOR SWIFT

She also has a cat named Meredith Grey, named after the character from   the TV show "Grey's Anatomy."

Taylor Swift is known for her philanthropy and has donated to various causes, including education and disaster relief.

She is an advocate for literacy and has donated books to schools and libraries.

Taylor Swift's album "1989" marked her transition to pop music

100 FACTS ABOUT TAYLOR SWIFT

She has a strong presence on social media, including Instagram, Twitter, and TikTok.

Taylor Swift often interacts with her fans on social media and shares   behind-the-scenes glimpses of her   life.

She has a close-knit group of friends   in the entertainment industry, known as the "Squad."

Taylor Swift has her own clothing line, Taylor Swift Style

100 FACTS ABOUT TAYLOR SWIFT

Taylor Swift's favorite number is 13, and she often incorporates it into her life and performances.

Taylor Swift's music videos are known for their elaborate storytelling and visuals.

Taylor Swift's song "Love Story" was inspired by William Shakespeare's "Romeo and Juliet."

She has a talent for creating catchy melodies.

100 FACTS ABOUT TAYLOR SWIFT

She is a strong advocate for artists' rights and has spoken out against music streaming services.

She has her own perfume line, including fragrances like "Wonderstruck" and "Taylor."

Taylor Swift is a talented songwriter, and many other artists have recorded songs she's written.

Taylor Swift is known for her impeccable sense of style and fashion.

100 FACTS ABOUT TAYLOR SWIFT

She has a strong presence in the fashion world and has graced the covers of many magazines.

Taylor Swift is known for her love of   baking, and she often shares her baking adventures on social media.

Taylor Swift has a song called "Bad Blood," which is rumored to be about a feud with another celebrity.

She has a strong work ethic and is dedicated to her music career.

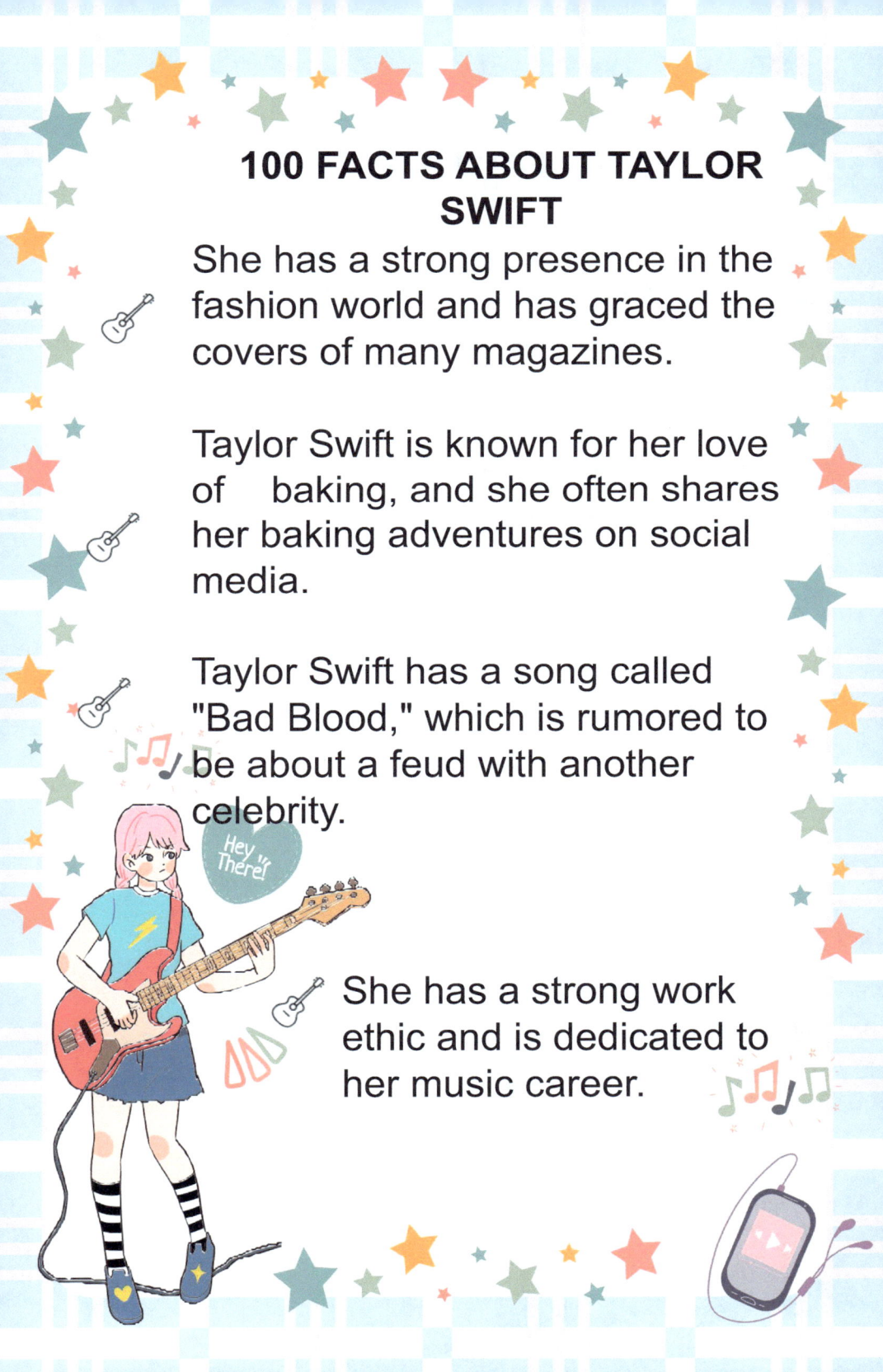

100 FACTS ABOUT TAYLOR SWIFT

She played the role of Bombalurina in   the movie adaptation of the musical "Cats."

Taylor Swift's song "Blank Space" is about the media's portrayal of her love life

Taylor Swift's album "Speak Now" features songs she wrote entirely by herself.

She is known for her generosity and often surprises fans with gifts and personal interactions.

100 FACTS ABOUT TAYLOR SWIFT

Taylor Swift has her own app, "The Swift Life," where fans can connect and share their love for her music.

She has a song called "Mine," which is about finding love unexpectedly.

Taylor Swift's song "All Too Well" is known for its emotional depth.

She is an advocate for body positivity and self-acceptance

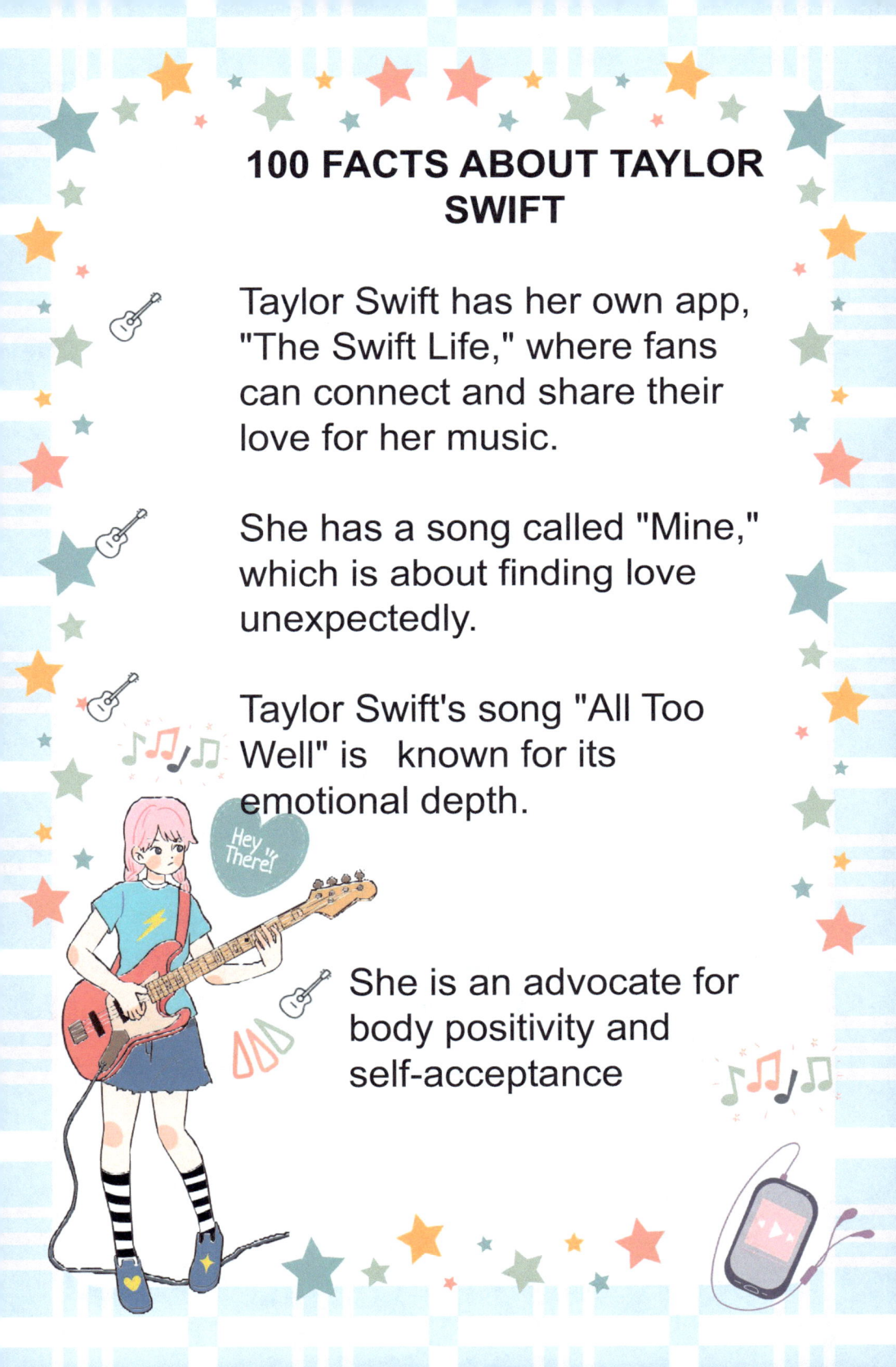

100 FACTS ABOUT TAYLOR SWIFT

Taylor Swift has a strong bond with her family and often mentions them   in interviews.

She has a song called "Wildest Dreams," which has a dreamy and romantic feel.

She is known for her red carpet looks and glamorous outfits.

Taylor Swift's song "I Knew You Were Trouble" is about a toxic relationship.

100 FACTS ABOUT TAYLOR SWIFT

She is an advocate for education and has donated to schools and educational programs.

Taylor Swift's song "The Story of Us" is about the ups and downs of a relationship.

She is known for her acoustic performances and intimate concerts

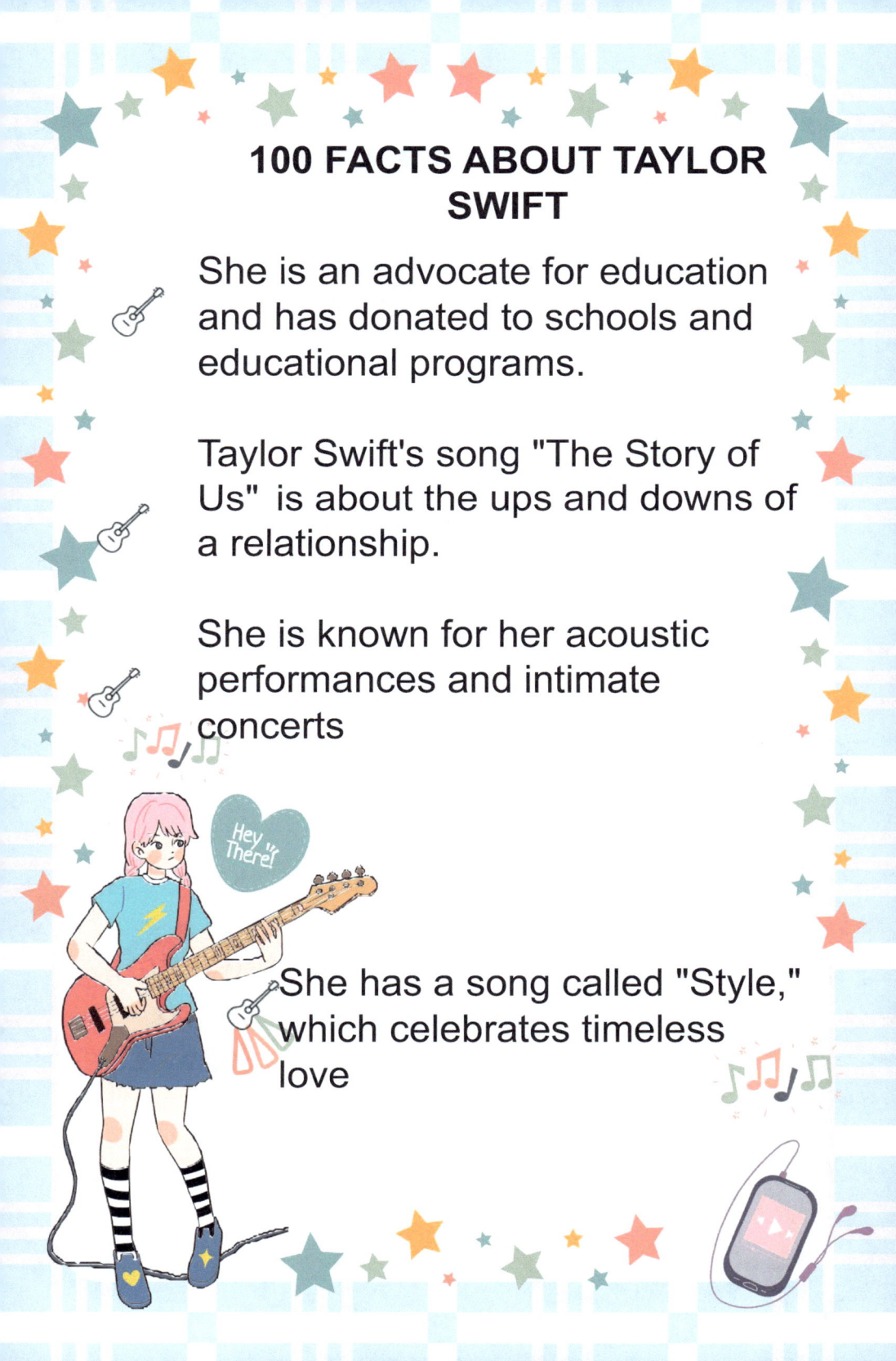

She has a song called "Style," which celebrates timeless love

100 FACTS ABOUT TAYLOR SWIFT

She is an ambassador for UNICEF and has travelled to help children in need.

She has a song called "Sparks Fly," which is about the excitement of falling in love.

Taylor Swift's song "Clean" is about moving on from a difficult experience.

She is a talented actress and has appeared in movies like "Valentine's

100 FACTS ABOUT TAYLOR SWIFT

Taylor Swift's song "Begin Again" is about finding love after heartbreak.

She is known for her songwriting workshops with fans.

She has a song called "Our Song," which is about a special shared   memory.

Taylor Swift's song "Fifteen" reflects on the challenges of growing up

100 FACTS ABOUT TAYLOR SWIFT

She has a song called "Long Live," which is a tribute to her fans.

Taylor Swift's song "Everything Has Changed" features British singer Ed Sheeran.

She is known for her colorful and creative music videos.

Taylor Swift's song "Red" captures the intensity of passionate love.

100 FACTS ABOUT TAYLOR SWIFT

She is an accomplished pianist and often plays piano during her live performances.

She has a song called "New Romantics," which celebrates a carefree spirit.

Taylor Swift's song "Back to December" is an apology to an ex-lover.

She is known for her love of vintage and retro fashion

100 FACTS ABOUT TAYLOR SWIFT

Taylor Swift's song "Should've Said No" is about betrayal in a relationship.

She is a strong advocate for women's rights and equality.

She has a song called "Change," which is about making a positive impact on the world.

She is known for her elaborate stage productions during her concert tours.

100 FACTS ABOUT TAYLOR SWIFT

She has a song called "Call It What You Want," which is about finding happiness in love.

Taylor Swift's song "All You Had to Do Was Stay" is about someone who walked away from a relationship.

She is a role model for many young girls, inspiring them to pursue their dreams.

Taylor Swift's song "Haunted" has a dark and mysterious vibe.

100 FACTS ABOUT TAYLOR SWIFT

She is known for her love of cats, and her cats often make appearances in   her social media posts.

She has a song called "Change," which is about overcoming obstacles.

Taylor Swift's song "The Last Great American Dynasty" tells the story of a controversial historical figure.

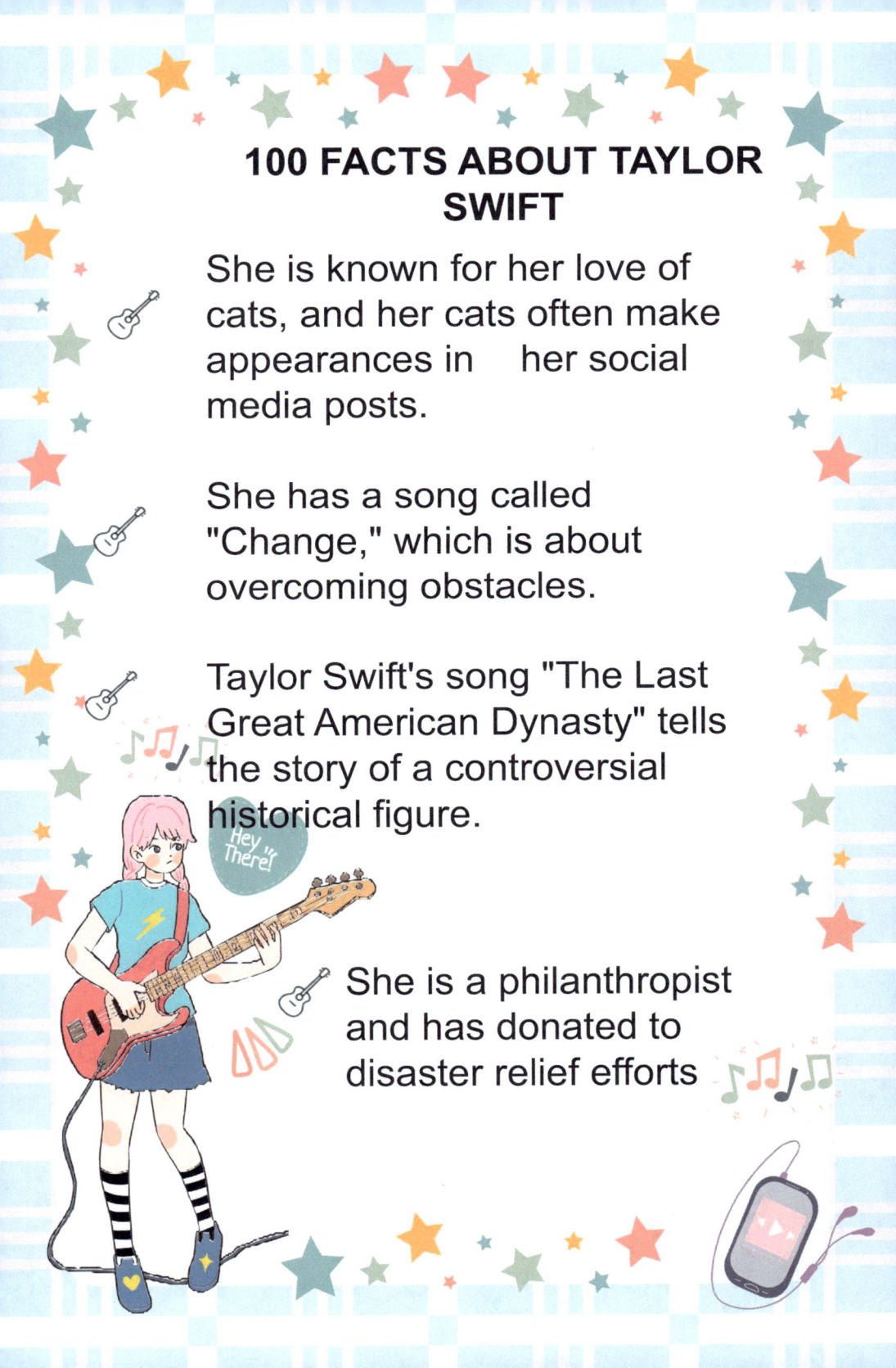

She is a philanthropist and has donated to disaster relief efforts

100 FACTS ABOUT TAYLOR SWIFT

She has a song called "Stay, Stay, Stay" which is about the joys of a happy relationship.

She is an advocate for animal rights and has supported animal rescue organizations.

She has a song called "White Horse," which is about the disappointment of a failed relationship.

She has a song called "Teardrops on My Guitar," which is about unrequited love.

100 FACTS ABOUT TAYLOR SWIFT

Taylor Swift has won numerous awards throughout her career, including multiple Grammy Awards.

Taylor Swift's album "Red" is known for its exploration of different emotions

She is a supporter of LGBTQ+ rights and has spoken out against discrimination

Taylor Swift is a big fan of cats and often shares cutecat videos and pictures

100 FACTS ABOUT TAYLOR SWIFT

She was the youngest artist to ever win the CMA Horizon Award (Country Music Association).

She has a song called "You Belong with Me," which many fans relate to.

She is a talented songwriter and has won the BMI Song of the Year award multiple times

Hey There!

She has a song called "22," which celebrates the joys of being 22 years old.

100 FACTS ABOUT TAYLOR SWIFT

She has a song called "Ours," which is about the beauty of love despite obstacles.

She has a fear of sea urchins. She once tweeted about it and even mentioned it in interviews, describing them as "alien creatures

Taylor Swift appeared in a humorous treadmill commercial for Apple Music,

100 FACTS ABOUT TAYLOR SWIFT

Taylor Swift's song "I Don't Wanna Live Forever" is a collaboration with Zayn Malik for the "Fifty Shades Darker" soundtrack.

She has a song called "Enchanted," which captures the feeling of meeting someone special.

Taylor Swift's song "Out of the Woods" explores the challenges of a relationship

100 FACTS ABOUT TAYLOR SWIFT

Taylor Swift had a supporting role in the 2014 film adaptation of the popular novel "The Giver" by Lois Lowry. She played the character Rosemary

She has a song called "Ronan," which is a tribute to a young boy who passed away from cancer.

Hey There!

She is known for her love of vintage and retro fashion

100 FACTS ABOUT TAYLOR SWIFT

Her music has touched the hearts of millions of fans around the world, and she continues to be a positive influence in the music industry.

Taylor Swift has performed the national anthem at several major sporting events, including the World Series and the Super Bowl.

She has a song called "Welcome to New York," which is an ode to the city

Taylor Swift Quotes…..

"The way I look at love is you have to follow it, and fall hard if you fall hard. You have to forget about what everyone else thinks."

"You are not the opinion of someone who doesn't know you."

"I've never been the type of woman who would not pick up the phone or not show up. That's always been a priority to me."

Taylor Swift Quotes.....

"The lesson I've learned the most often in life is that you're always going to know more in the future than you know now."

"In life, you learn lessons. And sometimes you learn them the hard way."

"Fearless is getting back up and fighting for what you want over and over again... even though every time you've tried before, you've lost."

"Just be yourself, there is no one better."

WORD SEARCH.1

```
U H T B C O K M R O N B B L H
B X N B A D G W B O Y W U A X
N M U S I C T L I T S V Y R S
C S S Y I R S T I R W L J O Z
M B C I E I A R E R I O N M Z
Z J H C N T B T B V F V Z A Z
U T N G U E I H M V T E M N S
B O E P L R E S F L I N V C I
C R E E W U S L Y M E J I E R
B R C G M E R R Y A S R T Y Q
P I N E L O T N L T Y F M F Q
P O W R L N F B S L S M P R D
S Z A Y U P U T Y A A O V E H
U E A O M M A M K R P B Q D A
F T C Y F C S D G L Q I Y H D
```

- [ ] ALBUM
- [ ] CATS
- [ ] CELEBRITY
- [ ] CONCERT
- [ ] COUNTRY
- [ ] FEARLESS
- [ ] GRAMMY
- [ ] LOVE
- [ ] LYRICS
- [ ] MUSIC
- [ ] POP
- [ ] RED
- [ ] REPUTATION
- [ ] ROMANCE
- [ ] SINGER
- [ ] SONGWRITER
- [ ] STYLE
- [ ] SWIFTIES
- [ ] TAYLOR

Maze

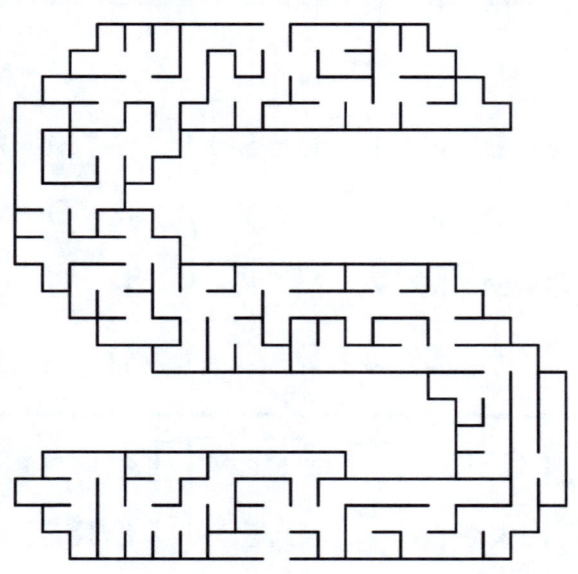

WORD SNAKE

```
U  B  H  Z  Q  M  L  E  L  R  A  R  A  M  M
U  G  R  A  R  Y  S  S  F  F  E  I  R  E  V
I  D  E  O  S  W  Y  N  S  "  E  H  I  L  O
T  C  K  I  W  E  S  E  H  A  N  A  C  B  V
A  M  A  F  T  I  G  P  A  K  E  I  R  N  E
R  L  A  C  B  I  R  M  Y  L  Y  T  J  U  S
U  P  H  I  L  L  A  M  S  E  P  O  "  N  O
F  A  R  G  B  O  A  R  "  R  U  F  F  G  S
N  O  S  O  I  A  U  D  C  "  T  P  S  T  Z
G  W  R  I  B  O  T  E  L  T  A  Y  S  O  R
R  K  S  T  E  R  B  D  L  I  C  R  E  T  Y
E  Y  "  9  8  A  S  T  I  O  O  T  L  L  G
O  J  "  1  9  P  O  H  V  N  U  N  H  I  N
G  S  I  C  R  R  P  N  H  "  O  F  "  "  E
F  T  N  G  E  B  Z  A  S  P  L  K  L  O  R
```

- [ ] "1989"
- [ ] "Folklore"
- [ ] "Lover"
- [ ] "Reputation"
- [ ] "Shake It Off"
- [ ] Americana
- [ ] Autobiographic
- [ ] Billboard
- [ ] Country
- [ ] Fearless
- [ ] Grammy
- [ ] Guitar
- [ ] Love Songs
- [ ] Nashville
- [ ] Pop
- [ ] Red
- [ ] Singer
- [ ] Songwriter
- [ ] Storytelling
- [ ] Swifties

WORD SEARCH - 2

```
W I C X E B B E L B B R M B L
M N P B K R N A S H V I L L E
Y S A N T H O P F A B I V O D
O P T W Q F V L I A Y Q T C M
S I D K A W O Y K K I B C M Z
L R Y C W R Y F Y L D A U Q S
S A G E E T D K V M O A F G D
F T H L N R U O T P T F U C F
L I Y E G X W F L R O I V A P
U O X B T B N N A D T Z Q A G
L N F R M E J H Q A U W H Q G
Z W E I J N C I R A G T U X V
E L M T X G M T N P U Q N N P
W L A Y P A C T R E S S K S S
O I F U S E R Z P A C V X D E
```

- [ ] ACTRESS
- [ ] CELEBRITY
- [ ] FAME
- [ ] GUITAR
- [ ] NASHVILLE
- [ ] TOUR
- [ ] AWARD
- [ ] CHART
- [ ] FOLKLORE
- [ ] INSPIRATION
- [ ] SQUAD

Test your knowledge about
Taylor Swift
Quiz

1. What is Taylor Swift's full name?
    a. Taylor Marie Swift
    b. Taylor Alison Swift
    c. Taylor Elizabeth Swift
    d. Taylor Nicole Swift

2. Which city was Taylor Swift born in?
    a. Nashville, Tennessee
    b. Reading, Pennsylvania
    c. Los Angeles, California
    d. New York City, New York

3. What was Taylor Swift's first single that became a hit?
    a. "Love Story"
    b. "Tim McGraw"
    c. "Blank Space"
    d. "Shake It Off"

Test your knowledge about
Taylor Swift
Quiz

4. Which of Taylor Swift's albums marked her transition to pop music?
   a. "Fearless"
   b. "Speak Now"
   c. "Red"
   d. "1989

5. Taylor Swift is known for her close-knit group of friends. What is this group often referred to as?
   a. The Squad
   b. The Clique
   c. The Swifties
   d. The Circle

Test your knowledge about
Taylor Swift
Quiz

6. Which song by Taylor Swift is rumoured to be about a feud with another celebrity?
   - a. "Love Story"
   - b. "Bad Blood"
   - c. "You Belong with Me"
   - d. "Mean"

7. Taylor Swift has won multiple awards, including numerous Grammy Awards. How many Grammy Awards has she won as of my last knowledge update in January 2022?
   - a. 5
   - b. 10
   - c. 15
   - d. 20

Test your knowledge about Taylor Swift
Quiz

8. Which of Taylor Swift's albums includes the hit single "Shake It Off"?
    a. "Fearless"
    b. "Speak Now"
    c. "Red"
    d. "1989"

9. In which year did Taylor Swift release her debut album?
    a. 2004
    b. 2006
    c. 2008
    d. 2010

10. What was the name of Taylor Swift's first concert tour?
    a. "Fearless Tour"
    b. "Red Tour"
    c. "Speak Now World Tour"
    d. "1989 World Tour"

Test your knowledge about
Taylor Swift
Quiz

11. Taylor Swift made her acting debut in which romantic comedy film?
    - a. "Valentine's Day"
    - b. "The Notebook"
    - c. "Crazy, Stupid, Love"
    - d. "The Proposal"

12. Which of the following awards did Taylor Swift receive at the age of 20, making her the youngest artist to ever win this award?
    - a. Academy Award (Oscar)
    - b. Nobel Prize in Literature
    - c. Grammy Award for Album of the Year
    - d. Presidential Medal of Freedom

Test your knowledge about Taylor Swift
Quiz

13. What is the title of Taylor Swift's song that tells the story of a tragic love affair and mentions Romeo and Juliet?
    a. "Love Story"
    b. "Blank Space"
    c. "You Belong with Me"
    d. "I Knew You Were Trouble"

14. Taylor Swift wrote a heartfelt song about a young boy named Ronan. What inspired this song?
    a. Her childhood memories
    b. A fictional story
    c. A tribute to a young cancer victim
    d. A breakup experience

15. What is the name of Taylor Swift's documentary film that offers a behind-the-scenes look at her life and career?
    a. "Fearless: The Taylor Swift Story"
    b. "Speak Now or Never"
    c. "Miss Americana"
    d. "1989 Uncovered"

16. Which Taylor Swift album features the track "We Are Never Ever Getting Back Together"?
    a. "Fearless"
    b. "Speak Now"
    c. "Red"
    d. "1989"

Test your knowledge about
Taylor Swift
Quiz

17. In 2019, Taylor Swift released an album that featured more introspective and indie-folk songs. What is the title of this album?
    a. "Reputation"
    b. "Lover"
    c. "Folklore"
    d. "Evermore"

18. Which of Taylor Swift's albums features songs she wrote entirely by herself?
    a. "Speak Now"
    b. "Fearless"
    c. "Red"
    d. "1989"

Test your knowledge about
Taylor Swift
Quiz

19. Taylor Swift is known for her love of cats. What are the names of her cats?
   - a. Whiskers and Mittens
   - b. Fluffy and Paws
   - c. Olivia Benson and Meredith Grey
   - d. Simba and Nala

20. What is Taylor Swift's favorite number, which she often incorporates into her life and performances?
   - a. 7
   - b. 13
   - c. 22
   - d. 1989

QUIZ ANSWERS

1. b. Taylor Alison Swift
2. b. Reading, Pennsylvania
3. b. "Tim McGraw"
4. d. "1989"
5. a. The Squad
6. b. "Bad Blood"
7. As of my last knowledge update in January 2022, the answer is c. 15 Grammy Awards, but please verify the current count.
8. a. "Speak Now"
9. c. Olivia Benson and Meredith Grey
10. b. 13
11. d. "1989"
12. b. 2006
13. a. "Fearless Tour"
14. a. "Valentine's Day"
15. c. Grammy Award for Album of the Year
16. a. "Love Story"
17. c. A tribute to a young cancer victim
18. c. "Miss Americana"
19. c. "Red"
20. c. "Folklore"

WORD SNAKE SOLUTION

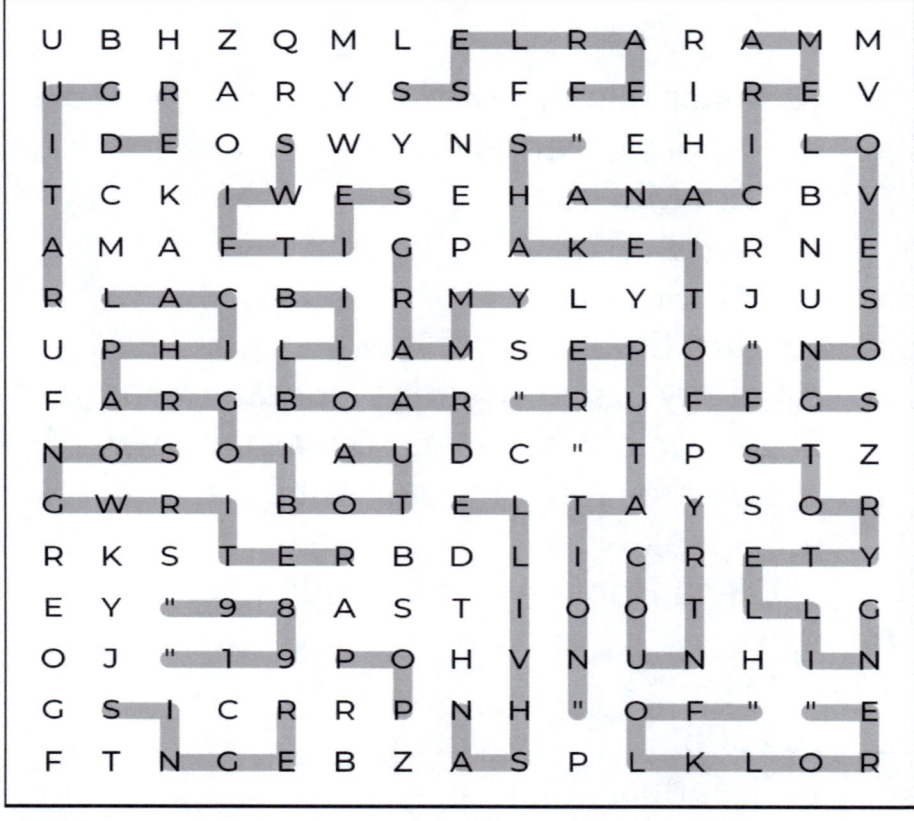

U B H Z Q M L E L R A R A M M
U G R A R Y S S F F E I R E V
I D E O S W Y N S " E H I L O
T C K I W E S E H A N A C B V
A M A F T I G P A K E I R N E
R L A C B I R M Y L Y T J U S
U P H I L L A M S E P O " N O
F A R G B O A R " R U F F G S
N O S O I A U D C " T P S T Z
G W R I B O T E L T A Y S O R
R K S T E R B D L I C R E T Y
E Y " 9 8 A S T I O O T L L G
O J " 1 9 P O H V N U N H I N
G S I C R R P N H " O F " " E
F T N G E B Z A S P L K L O R

- [ ] "1989"
- [ ] "Folklore"
- [ ] "Lover"
- [ ] "Reputation"
- [ ] "Shake It Off"
- [ ] Americana
- [ ] Autobiographic
- [ ] Billboard
- [ ] Country
- [ ] Fearless
- [ ] Grammy
- [ ] Guitar
- [ ] Love Songs
- [ ] Nashville
- [ ] Pop
- [ ] Red
- [ ] Singer
- [ ] Songwriter
- [ ] Storytelling
- [ ] Swifties

WORD SEARCH.1
SOLUTION

U	H	T	B	C	O	K	M	R	O	N	B	B	L	H
B	X	N	B	A	D	G	W	B	O	Y	W	U	A	X
N	M	U	S	I	C	T	L	I	T	S	V	Y	R	S
C	S	S	Y	I	R	S	T	I	R	W	L	J	O	Z
M	B	C	I	E	I	A	R	E	R	I	O	N	M	Z
Z	J	H	C	N	T	B	T	B	V	F	V	Z	A	Z
U	T	N	G	U	E	I	H	M	V	T	E	M	N	S
B	O	E	P	L	R	E	S	F	L	I	N	V	C	I
C	R	E	E	W	U	S	L	Y	M	E	J	I	E	R
B	R	C	G	M	E	R	R	Y	A	S	R	T	Y	Q
P	I	N	E	L	O	T	N	L	T	Y	F	M	F	Q
P	O	W	R	L	N	F	B	S	L	S	M	P	R	D
S	Z	A	Y	U	P	U	T	Y	A	A	O	V	E	H
U	E	A	O	M	M	A	M	K	R	P	B	Q	D	A
F	T	C	Y	F	C	S	D	G	L	Q	I	Y	H	D

- [ ] ALBUM
- [ ] CATS
- [ ] CELEBRITY
- [ ] CONCERT
- [ ] COUNTRY
- [ ] FEARLESS
- [ ] GRAMMY
- [ ] LOVE
- [ ] LYRICS
- [ ] MUSIC
- [ ] POP
- [ ] RED
- [ ] REPUTATION
- [ ] ROMANCE
- [ ] SINGER
- [ ] SONGWRITER
- [ ] STYLE
- [ ] SWIFTIES
- [ ] TAYLOR

WORD SEARCH.2
SOLUTION

```
W   I   C   X   E   B   B   E   L   B   B   R   M   B   L
M   N   P   B   K   R   N   A   S   H   V   I   L   L   E
Y   S   A   N   T   H   O   P   F   A   B   I   V   O   D
O   P   T   W   Q   F   V   L   I   A   Y   Q   T   C   M
S   I   D   K   A   W   O   Y   K   K   I   B   C   M   Z
L   R   Y   C   W   R   Y   F   Y   L   D   A   U   Q   S
S   A   G   E   E   T   D   K   V   M   O   A   F   G   D
F   T   H   L   N   R   U   O   T   P   T   F   U   C   F
L   I   Y   E   G   X   W   F   L   R   O   I   V   A   P
U   O   X   B   T   B   N   N   A   D   T   Z   Q   A   G
L   N   F   R   M   E   J   H   Q   A   U   W   H   Q   G
Z   W   E   I   J   N   C   I   R   A   G   T   U   X   V
E   L   M   T   X   G   M   T   N   P   U   Q   N   N   P
W   L   A   Y   P   A   C   T   R   E   S   S   K   S   S
O   I   F   U   S   E   R   Z   P   A   C   V   X   D   E
```

- [ ] ACTRESS
- [ ] AWARD
- [ ] CELEBRITY
- [ ] CHART
- [ ] FAME
- [ ] FOLKLORE
- [ ] GUITAR
- [ ] INSPIRATION
- [ ] NASHVILLE
- [ ] SQUAD
- [ ] TOUR

A Special Note to Our Young Readers:

As we turn the final page of this journey through Taylor Swift's inspiring life and career, we want to extend a heartfelt thank you to each of you for joining us. Taylor's story is more than just a tale of fame and music; it's a testament to the power of dreaming big, working hard, and staying true to oneself.

A Special Note to Our Young Readers:

We hope that as you explored her biography, delved into the fun facts, solved puzzles, aced quizzes, and brought color to the pages, you found more than just entertainment. May these stories and activities have sparked a sense of creativity, determination, and confidence within you.

A Special Note to Our Young Readers:

Remember, every one of you is unique and capable of writing your own incredible story. Whether you dream of standing on a stage, inventing something new, helping others, or whatever your heart desires, believe in yourself as fiercely as Taylor believes in her music.

A Special Note to Our Young Readers:

As Taylor Swift has shown us, life is a beautiful and sometimes challenging melody. Embrace it, sing it your way, and never forget that you have the strength and courage to achieve your dreams.

Wishing you all the best on your journey ahead.

With Love,   Brooke Stone

Manufactured by Amazon.ca
Bolton, ON

37972891R00044